DEDICATION

TO:

FROM:

I wish for you a life of wealth, health, and happiness; a life in which you give to yourself the gift of patience, the virtue of reason, the value of knowledge, and the influence of faith in your own ability to dream about and to achieve worthy rewards.

Jim Rohn

THE TREASURY OF QUOTES
BY JIM ROHN

Features 365 quotes on 60
topics gathered over 30
years of wit and wisdom
from Jim Rohn.

Burgundy hardback with
gold foil lettering.
Retail $20 each
Special $12 each

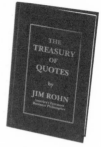

Call 800-929-0434
Visit us at jimrohn.com
(sign up for FREE E-zine)

EXCERPTS FROM
THE TREASURY OF QUOTES

These booklets from Jim Rohn and Brian Tracy contain
a special **TO...and FROM...**section.

*Makes a great gift or addition to any thank you
or holiday card. Perfect for customers, family
and friends!*

MIX AND MATCH PRICING
SEE BACK PAGE
FOR
ORDERING INFORMATION

Excerpts from

THE TREASURY OF QUOTES

This booklet contains 134 quotes from Jim Rohn's book, "The Treasury of Quotes," a collection of 365 quotes gathered from Jim Rohn's personal journals, seminars and books (see opposite page). These quotes reflect over 39 years of experience in business and in sharing ideas and affecting people's lives.

To date, Jim Rohn's message has reached an audience of over 4 million people. May Jim's words now affect you, your family, friends, and business associates as you feast upon this sampling which has been taken directly from his magnificent treasury of life-changing ideas and inspiration.

WHAT OTHERS ARE SAYING
ABOUT JIM ROHN...

"Jim is one of the most articulate, powerful, thought provoking speakers I've seen. His unique delivery and style put him head and shoulders above the rest."

Harvey Mackay, Author, "Swim with the Sharks Without Being Eaten Alive"

"Jim Rohn is outstanding! He is among the most polished, professional speakers in America, with a message everyone should hear."

Brian Tracy, President of Brian Tracy Learning Systems

"Jim Rohn, my first personal development teacher, always taught me that if you have enough reasons, you can do anything. Reasons are the difference between being interested versus being committed to accomplish something."

Anthony Robbins, from his book "Unlimited Power"

"Jim Rohn is a modern day Will Rogers. His perceptions of achievement and success have launched thousands of people on a wonderful life-changing voyage into success and happiness. I can't recommend too strongly that you experience Jim Rohn personally."

Tom Hopkins, President of Tom Hopkins International

"I've been a student of Jim Rohn since our days with Bestline Products. He was then and still is one of the most profound thinkers and mind expanding individuals I've ever had a chance to listen to."

Les Brown, Author, "Live Your Dreams"

ISBN 0-939490-05-6

PERSONAL DEVELOPMENT

Unless you change how you are, you will always have what you've got.

Life is a unique combination of "want to" and "how to," and we need to give equal attention to both.

The most important question to ask on the job is not "What am I getting?" The most important question to ask is "What am I becoming?"

Pity the man who inherits a million dollars and isn't a millionaire. Here's what would be pitiful, if your income grew and you didn't.

We can have more than we've got because we can become more than we are.

LEADERSHIP/MANAGEMENT

The challenge of leadership is to be strong, but not rude. Be kind, but not weak. Be bold, but not a bully. Be thoughtful, but not lazy. Be humble, but not timid. Be proud, but not arrogant. Have humor, but without folly.

Sometimes those who need it the most are inclined the least.

My mentor said, "Let's go do it" not "You go do it." How powerful when someone says, "Let's!"

Good people are found, not changed. Recently I read a headline that said, "We don't teach our people to be nice. We simply hire nice people." Wow! What a clever short cut.

A good objective of leadership is to help those who are doing poorly to do well and to help those who are doing well to do even better.

4

LEADERSHIP/MANAGEMENT

If you share a good idea long enough, it will eventually fall on good people.

Leadership is the challenge to be something more than average.

Leaders, whether in the family, in business, in government, or in education, must not allow themselves to mistake intentions for accomplishments.

Leaders must learn to discipline their disappointments. It is not what happens to us, it is what we choose to do about what happens that makes the difference in how our lives turn out.

Learn to help people with more than just their jobs; help them with their lives.

In leadership we teach: Don't send your ducks to eagle school because it won't help. Duck finishes eagle school, sees his first rabbit, makes him a friend.

5

ACTIVITY/LABOR

Life responds to deserve and not to need. It doesn't say, "If you need, you will reap." It says, "If you plant you will reap." The guy says, "I really need to reap." Then you really need to plant.

The few who do are the envy of the many who only watch.

Make rest a necessity, not an objective. Only rest long enough to gather strength.

The soil says, "Don't bring me your need. Bring me your seed."

You must learn to translate wisdom and strong feelings into labor.

You must get good at one of two things: planting in the spring or begging in the fall.

6

DESIRE/MOTIVATION

Humans have the remarkable ability to get exactly what they must have. But there is a difference between a "must" and a "want."

The best motivation is self-motivation. The guy says, "I wish someone would come by and turn me on." What if they don't show up? You've got to have a better plan for your life.

When you know what you want, and you want it badly enough, you'll find a way to get it.

Motivation alone is not enough. If you have an idiot and you motivate him, now you have a motivated idiot.

If you wish to find, you must search. Rarely does a good idea interrupt you.

Without a sense of urgency, desire loses its value.

KNOWLEDGE/EDUCATION

Learning is the beginning of wealth. Learning is the beginning of health. Learning is the beginning of spirituality. Searching and learning is where the miracle process all begins.

Formal education will make you a living. Self-education will make you a fortune.

We must learn to apply all that we know so that we can attract all that we want.

The book you don't read won't help.

If someone is going down the wrong road, he doesn't need motivation to speed him up. What he needs is education to turn him around.

Some people read so little they have rickets of the mind.

KNOWLEDGE/EDUCATION

Miss a meal if you have to, but don't miss a book.

The great gift of the human imagination is that it has no limits or ending.

Nourish the mind like you would your body. The mind cannot survive on junk food.

Everything you need for your better future and success has already been written. And guess what? It's all available. All you have to do is go to the library. But guess what? Only three percent of the people in America have a library card. Wow, they must be expensive! No, they're free. Probably in every neighborhood. Three percent!

Ignorance is <u>not</u> bliss. Ignorance is poverty. Ignorance is devastation. Ignorance is tragedy. Ignorance is illness. It all stems from ignorance.

RESULTS/SUCCESS

Success is not to be pursued; it is to be attracted by the person we become.

At the end of each day you should play back the tapes of your performance. The results should either applaud you or prod you.

There are some things you don't have to know how it works. The main thing is that it works. While some people are studying the roots, others are picking the fruit. It just depends which end of this you want to get in on.

Part of success is preparation on purpose.

If you care at all, you'll get some results. If you care enough, you'll get incredible results.

Success is not so much what we have as it is what we are.

RESULTS/SUCCESS

The greatest form of maturity is at harvest time. That is when we must learn how to reap without complaint if the amounts are small and how to to reap without apology if the amounts are big.

My goal is to translate response into results. Some teachers teach for others to learn. That's not me. Some teachers teach for others to accomplish. That is me.

Life asks us to make measurable progress in reasonable time. That's why they make those fourth grade chairs so small.

Success is the study of the obvious. Everyone should take Obvious 1 and Obvious 2 in school.

I found it easier to get rich than I did to make excuses.

GOALS/PLANS

Goals. There's no telling what you can do when you get inspired by them. There's no telling what you can do when you believe in them. There's no telling what will happen when you act upon them.

Reasons come first. Answers come second.

There are two ways to face the future. One way is with apprehension; the other is with anticipation.

The guy says, "When you work where I work, by the time you get home it's late. You've got to have a bite to eat, watch a little TV, relax, and get to bed. You can't sit up half the night planning, planning, planning." And he's the same guy who's behind on his car payment.

When the promise is clear, the price gets easy.

GOALS/PLANS

I find it fascinating that most people plan their vacations with better care than they do their lives. Perhaps that is because escape is easier than change.

If you go to work on your goals, your goals will go to work on you. If you go to work on your plan, your plan will go to work on you. Whatever good things we build end up building us.

We all need lots of powerful long-range goals to help us past the short-term obstacles.

We must be careful not to let our current appetites steal away any chance we might have for a future feast.

We all have two choices: We can make a living or we can design a life.

13

TIME/TIME MANAGEMENT

Time is our most valuable asset, yet we tend to waste it, kill it, and spend it rather than invest it.

We can no more afford to spend major time on minor things than we can to spend minor time on major things.

The greatest definition for concentration I ever heard is, "Wherever you are, be there!"

You don't get paid for the hour. You get paid for the value you bring to an hour.

Time is more valuable than money. You can get more money, but you can't get more time.

Never begin the day until it is finished on paper.

LIFESTYLE

Learn how to be happy with what you have while you pursue all that you want.

Happiness is not an accident. Nor is it something you wish for. Happiness is something you design.

There are three things to leave behind: your photographs, your library, and your personal journals. These things are certainly going to be more valuable to future generations than your furniture!

The word "tip" stands for "to insure promptness." So when should you give it? Up front, of course. Sophisticated people don't take chances on poor service, they insure good service.

Let others lead small lives, but not you. Let others argue over small things, but not you. Let others cry over small hurts, but not you. Let others leave their future in someone else's hands, but not you.

15

AMERICA/GOVERNMENT/POLITICS

It can be dangerous to weaken the strong in our attempts to strengthen the weak.

One of the great liberal documents of the world is the Declaration of Independence. One of the great conservative documents of the world is the Constitution of the United States. We need both documents to build a country. One to get it started. Liberal. And the other to help maintain its structure over the years. Conservative.

The real genius to make a marketplace flourish doesn't come from the government. It comes from the individual genius of its people.

Beware of those who seek to take care of you lest your caretakers become your jailers.

An ancient script asks, "Would you let a man rule the city who cannot even rule his own spirit?" Sometimes we do.

AMERICA/GOVERNMENT/POLITICS

In America we have the greatest chance for opportunity than anyone else in the past six and a half thousand years. Never in recorded history have so many different gifts been brought from all over the world and deposited in one country.

Debate refines a good idea. That's why we have two major parties in Congress. Somebody says, "I have a great idea for the country." We say, "Wonderful. Put it on the table. Let's debate." And we start the debate by questioning the guy who has this great idea. After the third question he says, "I withdraw my great idea. I forgot about those three questions."

Succeeding in America is easy! That's why everyone wants to come here. People haven't plotted and schemed for the last fifty years saying, "If I could just get to Poland everything would be okay."

Tyranny knows no restraint of appetite.

17

BUSINESS/CAREER/MARKETPLACE

My father taught me always to do more than you get paid for as an investment in your future.

If you make a sale you make a living. If you make an investment of time and good service in a customer, you can make a fortune.

Don't just let your business or your job make something for you, let it make something of you.

The worst days of those who enjoy what they do are better than the best days of those who don't.

One good customer well taken care of could be more valuable than $10,000 worth of advertising.

Don't bring your need to the marketplace, bring your skill. If you don't feel well, tell your doctor but not the marketplace. If you need money, go to your bank but not the marketplace.

18

RESOLVE/BELIEF/ASKING

Asking is the beginning of receiving. Make sure you don't go to the ocean with a teaspoon. At least take a bucket so the kids won't laugh at you.

If you are not willing to risk the unusual, you will have to settle for the ordinary.

There is no better opportunity to receive more than to be thankful for what you already have. Thanksgiving opens up the windows of opportunity for ideas to flow your way.

We must risk going too far to discover just how far we can go.

Resolve says, "I will." The man says, "I will climb this mountain. They told me it is too high, too far, too steep, too rocky, and too difficult. But it's my mountain. I will climb it. You will soon see me waving from the top or dead on the side from trying."

19

SKILLS/FUNDAMENTALS

Success is neither magical nor mysterious. Success is the natural consequence of consistently applying basic fundamentals.

There are only about a half dozen things that make 80% of the difference in any area of our lives.

Don't wish it were easier; wish you were better. Don't wish for less problems; wish for more skills. Don't wish for less challenges; wish for more wisdom.

Learn to hide your need and show your skill.

Success is nothing more than a few simple disciplines, practiced every day, while failure is simply a few errors in judgement, repeated every day. It is the accumulative weight of our disciplines and our judgements that leads us to either fortune or failure.

CHOICE/CHANGE/DECISION

Don't say, "If I could, I would." Say instead, "If I can, I will."

It is our philosophical set of the sail that determines the course of our lives. To change our current direction, we have to change our philosophy not our circumstances.

I used to say, "I sure hope things will change." Then I learned that the only way things are going to change for me is when I change.

Disgust and resolve are two of the great emotions that lead to change.

We generally change ourselves for one of two reasons: inspiration or desperation.

If you don't like where you are, change it! You're not a tree.

FEAR/DOUBT/NEGATIVITY

One of the reasons many people don't have what they want is neglect. Neglect starts out as an infection and then develops into a disease.

We must all wage an intense, lifelong battle against the constant downward pull. If we relax, the bugs and the weeds of negativity will move into the garden and take away everything of value.

If you spend five minutes complaining, you have just wasted five minutes. If you continue complaining, it won't be long before they haul you out to a financial desert and there let you choke on the dust of your own regret.

Humility is a virtue; timidity is an illness.

Self-preservation has a tendency to lead to poverty.

INFLUENCE/ASSOCIATION

Don't join an easy crowd. You won't grow. Go where the expectations and the demands to perform are high.

There are two parts to influence. First, influence is powerful. And second, it is subtle. You wouldn't let someone push you off course, but you might let someone nudge you off course and not even realize it.

You must constantly ask yourself these questions: Who am I around? What are they doing to me? What have they got me reading? What have they got me saying? Where do they have me going? What do they have me thinking? And most important, what do they have me becoming? Then ask yourself the big question: Is that okay?

Let the views of others educate and inform you, but let your decisions be a product of your own conclusions.

23

COMMUNICATION/PERSUASION

You cannot speak that which you do not know. You cannot share that which you do not feel. You cannot translate that which you do not have. And you cannot give that which you do not possess. To give it and to share it, and for it to be effective you first need to have it. Good communication starts with good preparation.

The goal of effective communication should be for the listener to say, "Me, too!" versus "So what?"

For effective communication, use brevity. Jesus said, "Follow me." Now that's brief! He could be brief because of all that he was that he didn't have to say.

What is powerful is when what you say is just the tip of the iceberg of what you know.

If you just communicate you can get by. But if you skillfully communicate, you can work miracles.

24

KIDS

Kids are curious. Kids are watching ants while adults are stepping on them.

Kids ought to have two bicycles: one to ride and one to rent.

Of course kids should pay taxes. Tell little Johnny if he wants to ride his bicycle on the sidewalk instead of in the mud, he's got to pay 3 more pennies when he buys a candy bar.

Kids don't lack capacity, only teachers.

Here's what we must teach our children in the '90s - the skill of selective listening. Don't spend most of your time on the voices that don't count, voices that are going to add too little worth to your future. Don't waste time on the shallow and the silly. Tune those voices out and tune in the voices that are going to add something to your life.

FINANCES/WEALTH

The philosophy of the rich versus the poor is this: The rich invest their money and spend what's left; the poor spend their money and invest what's left.

To become financially independent you must turn part of your income into capital; turn capital into enterprise; turn enterprise into profit; turn profit into investment; and turn investment into financial independence.

If you are not financially independent by the time you are forty or fifty, it doesn't mean that you are living in the wrong country or at the wrong time. It simply means that you have the wrong plan.

I used to say, "Things cost too much." Then my teacher straightened me out on that by saying, "The problem isn't that things cost too much. The problem is that you can't afford it." That's when I finally understood that the problem wasn't it - the problem was me!

RELATIONSHIPS

One person caring about another represents life's greatest value.

Your family and your love must be cultivated like a garden. Time, effort, and imagination must be summoned constantly to keep it flourishing and growing.

The greatest gift you can give to somebody is your own personal development. I used to say, "If you will take care of me, I will take care of you." Now I say, "I will take care of me for you, if you will take care of you for me."

The walls we build around us to keep out the sadness also keep out the joy.

You cannot succeed by yourself. It's hard to find a rich hermit.

MOTIVATION

(a special excerpt from the
Challenge to Succeed Seminar)

Motivation is a mystery. Why does one salesperson see his first prospect at seven in the morning and another salesperson is just getting out of bed at eleven? I don't know. It's part of the mysteries of life.

Give a lecture to a thousand people. One walks out and says, "I'm going to change my life." Another one walks out with a yawn and says, "I've heard all this before." Why is that? Why wouldn't both be affected the same way? Another mystery.

The millionaire says to a thousand people, "I read this book and it started me on the road to wealth." Guess how many go out and get the book? Very few. Isn't that incredible? Why wouldn't everyone get the book? A mystery of life.

My suggestion would be to walk away from the 90% who don't and join the 10% who do.

JIM ROHN:
AMERICA'S FOREMOST
BUSINESS PHILOSOPHER

For more than 39 years Jim Rohn has focused on the fundamentals of human behavior that most affect personal and business performance. Jim is the standard to which those who seek to teach and inspire others are compared. He possesses the unique ability to bring extraordinary insights to ordinary principles and events, and the combination of his substance and style captures the imagination of those who hear or read his words.

Having established his fortune and reputation as the head of several business enterprises, he now concentrates his creative skills on Jim Rohn International, a diversified corporation engaged in the worldwide marketing of personal development, management, and sales-oriented seminars and training programs.

Jim Rohn has now shared his message with over 6,000 audiences and 4 million people. He has conducted his

seminars and workshops throughout Europe, Asia, Australia and Africa, as well as in most principal cities in North America.

Jim is a member of the National Speakers Association and a recipient of its coveted CPAE Award, given to him in 1985 for outstanding performance and professionalism in speaking.